This edition first published in 2017 by Conari Press
an imprint of Red Wheel/Weiser, LLC
With offices at:
65 Parker Street, Suite 7
Newburyport, MA 01950
www.redwheelweiser.com

Editorial selection, arrangement, and design copyright © 2015 Helen Exley Creative Ltd.
Illustrations by Angela Kerr copyright © 2015 Helen Exley Creative Ltd.
The publishers are grateful for permission to reproduce copyright material.
While every effort has been made to trace copyright holders, we would be pleased
to hear from any not here acknowledged. The moral right of the author has been asserted.

ISBN 978-1-57324-725-2

Library of Congress Cataloging-in-Publication Data available upon request

Printed in China.

HE

12 11 10 9 8 7 6 5 4 3 2 1

THE GIFT OF
GREAT
CHINESE
WISDOM

ILLUSTRATIONS BY ANGELA KERR
EDITED BY HELEN EXLEY

Conari Press

Knowing others
is intelligence;
knowing yourself
is true wisdom.
Mastering others
is strength;
mastering yourself
is true power.

LAO TZU   6TH CENTURY B.C.

Internal Peace

Only those who know internal peace
can give it to others.

LAO TZU 6TH CENTURY B.C.

Whenever you hear that someone else
has been successful, rejoice.
Always practice rejoicing for others –
whether your friend or your enemy.
If you cannot practice rejoicing, no matter
how long you live, you will not be happy.

LAO TZU 6ᵀᴴ CENTURY B.C.

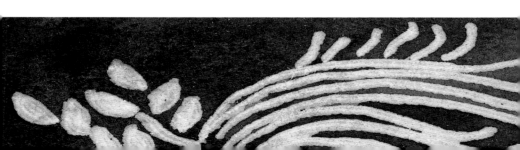

joicing

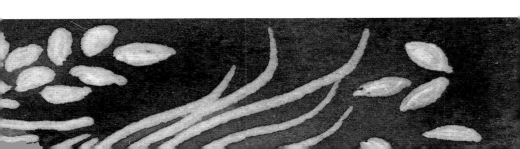

The one who knows does not speak.
The one who speaks does not know.

LAO TZU 6TH CENTURY B.C.

Your own body is not your possession...
It is the shape lent to you by heaven and earth.
Your life is not your possession; it is harmony between
your forces, granted for a time by heaven and earth.
Your nature and destiny are not your possessions;
they are the course laid down for you by heaven
and earth. Your children and grandchildren
are not your possessions; heaven and earth lend
them to you to cast off from you body as an insect
sheds its skin. Therefore you travel without knowing
where you go, stay without knowing
what you cling to, are fed without knowing how.
You are the breath of heaven and earth which goes
to and fro; how can you ever possess it?

LAO TZU 6TH CENTURY B.C.

A journey
of a thousand miles must begin
with a single step.

LAO TZU 6ᵀᴴ CENTURY B.C.

Help others
for all the times that
you have been ignored.
Be kind to others,
for all the times you
have been scorned.

DENG MING-DAO

What life can compare to this?
Sitting quietly by the window,
I watch the leaves fall
and the flowers bloom,
as the seasons come and go.

HSUEH TOU 982-1052

There is nothing under the canopy of heaven
greater than the tip of a bird's down.

CHUANG TZU 369-286 B.C.

I<small>f</small> you keep a green bough
in your heart,
the singing bird will come.

CHINESE PROVERB

The best
fighters display
no anger.
The best
conqueror seeks
no revenge.

LAO TZU   6TH CENTURY B.C.

Manifest plainness,
Embrace simplicity,
Reduce selfishness,
Have few desires.

LAO TZU   6TH CENTURY B.C.

In doing good, avoid fame. In doing bad, avoid disgrace. Pursue a middle course as your principle. Thus you will guard your body from harm, preserve your life, fulfil your duties by your parents, and live your allotted span of life.

CHUANG TZU 369-286 B.C.

The best person is like water.
Water is good; it benefits all things
and does not compete with them.
It dwells in lowly
places that all disdain.

TAO TE CHING

Being Here

Without stirring abroad one can know
the whole world; Without looking out of the window
one can see the way of heaven.
The further one goes the less one knows.

CHUANG TZU 369-286 B.C.

THE GREATEST REVELATION IS STILLNESS.

LAO TZU 6TH CENTURY B.C.

When I dig another person
out of trouble,
the hole from which I lift him
is the place where I bury my own.

CHINESE PROVERB

If you realize that you have

enough, you are truly rich.

TAO TE CHING

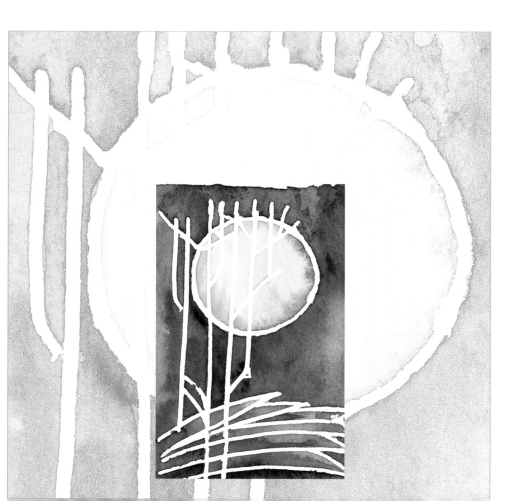

As soon as you have made a thought, laugh at it.

LAO TZU
6TH CENTURY B.C.

SILENCE IS A SOURCE

OF GREAT STRENGTH.

LAO TZU 6TH CENTURY B.C.

He who deliberates fully before taking a step will spend his entire life on one leg.

CHINESE PROVERB

Is there one maxim
which ought to be acted upon
throughout one's whole life?
Surely it is the maxim
of loving kindness:
Do not unto others
what you would not
have them do unto you.

CONFUCIUS 551-479 B.C.

Never give way to anger
otherwise in one day
you could burn up the wood
that you collected
in many bitter weeks.

MENG TSE

If you don't know where you're going, any road will take you there.

CHINESE PROVERB

To lead the people, wal

When the best leader's work is done
people say, "We did it ourselves".

ehind them.

LAO TZU 6TH CENTURY B.C.

When my heart is at peace
the world is at peace.

ZEN POEM

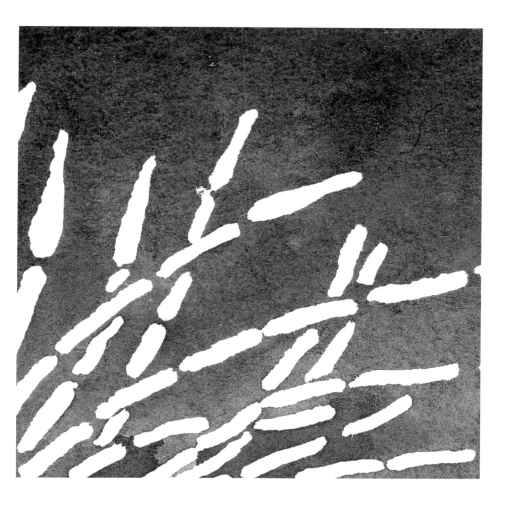

Choose a job you love,
and you will never
have to work a day
in your life.

CONFUCIUS 551-479 B.C.

Never
has a person
who is bent
been able
to make others
straight.

MENCIUS 372-289 B.C.

Life is a series of natural
and spontaneous changes.
Don't resist them -
that only creates sorrow.
Let reality be reality.
Let things flow naturally forward
in whatever way they will.

TAO TE CHING

Seize every minute

Seize every minute
Of your time.
The days fly by;
Ere long you too
Will grow old.

TZU YEH (256-316) TSIN DYNASTY

The great man
is he who does not
lose his
child's heart.

MENCIUS 372- 289 B.C.

Every smile
makes you
a day younger;
every sigh
a day older.

CHINESE PROVERB

Always we hope someone else
has the answer.
Some other place will be better,
some other time it will all turn out.
This is it.
No one else has the answer.
No other place will be better,
and it has already turned out.

No on

LAO TZU 6TH CENTURY B.C.

lse has the answer…

HAVE MUCH AND BE CONFUSED.

LAO TZU 6TH CENTURY B.C.

The best soldier
does not attack.
The superior fighter succeeds
without violence.
The greatest conqueror wins
without struggle.
The most successful manager
leads without dictating.

TAO TE CHING

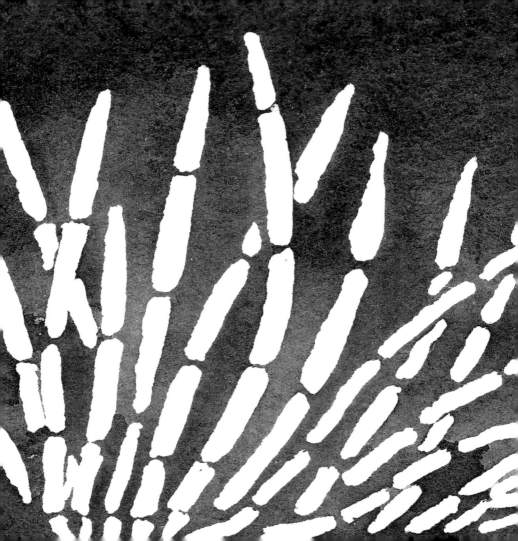

Our greatest glory
is not in never falling,
but in rising
every time we fall.

CONFUCIUS 551-479 B.C.

If you're not pure and not sincere, you can't move people. Fake tears and wailing may appear sorrowful, but they don't make real mourning. Fake anger may make you stern, but it doesn't produce awe. Fake affection, and you'll get smiles, but no harmony.

True sorrow can mourn without
a sound. True anger can be awesome
even before it's visible.
True affection brings harmony even
before it brings a smile. When truth
is inside, the spirit can move abroad.
That's the noble value of truth.

CHUANG TZU 369-286 B.C.

CHANGELESSNESS IS DEATH.

CHINESE PROVERB

Those who know that enough
is enough will always have enough.

LAO TZU 6TH CENTURY B.C.

Only the forest and I

We sat together,
the forest and I,
merging into silence.
Until only
the forest remained.

LI PO 701-762

To the mind
that is still,
the whole
universe
surrenders.

LAO TZU 6TH CENTURY B.C.

Grant yourself a moment of peace
and you will understand how foolishly
you have scurried about.
Learn to be silent and you will notice
that you have talked too much.

TSCHEN TSCHI JU

To be uncert[ain]
is to be
uncomfortab[le]
but to be
certain is to [be]
ridiculous.

CHINESE WISDO[M]

Why do you scorn others?
Can it be that
you are that proud?
No matter how
accomplished you are,
there are people ahead
of you and behind you.

DENG MING-DAO

To have enough is happiness,
to have more than enough is harmful.
That is true of all things,
but especially of money.

LAO TZU 6TH CENTURY B.C.

A good traveller
has no fixed plans
and is not
intent on arriving.

LAO TZU 6TH CENTURY B.C.

The path of duty lies in what is near,
and people seek for it in what is remote;
the work of duty lies in what is easy,
and people seek for it in what is difficult.

MENCIUS 372- 289 B.C.

Only a wise person can unite the quickness, clarity, breadth and depth of understanding needed for guiding others; the magnanimity, generosity, benevolence, and gentleness needed for getting along with others, the serenity, seriousness, unwaveringness and the well-informedness and thoroughness needed for exercising sound judgement.

CONFUCIUS 551 - 479 B.C.

ANYONE
WHO PILES
UP TREASURE
HAS MUCH
TO LOSE.

LAO TZU 6TH CENTURY B.C.

Stillness is joy. Joy is free from care.
Fruitful in long years. Joy does all things
without concern: For emptiness,
stillness, tranquillity, tastelessness, silence
and non-action are the root of all things.

CHUANG TZU 369-286 B.C.

THE GREAT PERSON IS SPARING
IN WORDS
BUT PRODIGAL IN DEEDS.

CONFUCIUS 551-479 B.C.

Iɴ A HUNDRED MILE MARCH,
NINETY IS ABOUT THE HALFWAY POINT.

CHINESE PROVERB

W̲e must decide on what we will not do,
and then we will be able to act
with vigour in what we ought to do.

MENCIUS 372-289 B.C.

OUTSIDE NOISY, INSIDE

CHINESE SAYING

MPTY.

When eating bamboo sprouts,
remember the person who planted them.

CHINESE PROVERB

To be the best person be careful of these things:
...Your face that it may always reflect kindness;
Your manners that they might show
respect for other people;
Your words that they may be true;
Your dealings with
other people that they may be fair.

CONFUCIUS 551-479 B.C.

So if loss of what gives
happiness causes you distress
when it fades, you
can now understand that
such happiness is worthless.

CHUANG TZU 369-286 B.C.

In Chinese,
the symbol for the word
"crisis" has two meanings:
danger and opportunity.

DOUGLAS KENNEDY

Thorns spring up when an army passes.
Years of misery follow a great victory.

TAO TE CHING

One

The universe
and I came into being together;
and I and everything
therein are one.

CHUANG TZU 369-286 B.C.

Letting it go

By letting it go it all gets done. The world is won by those who let it go. But when you try and try, the world is beyond the winning.

LAO TZU
6TH CENTURY B.C.

A tree that is unbending is easily broken.

LAO TZU 6TH CENTURY B.C.

"If it were just a matter of playing football with the firmament, stirring up the ocean, turning back rivers, carrying away mountains, seizing the moon, moving the Pole-star or shifting a planet, I could manage it easily enough. Even if it were a question

of my head being cut off and the brain
removed or my belly being ripped open
and my heart cut out... I would take
on the job at once," said Monkey.
"But if it comes to sitting still and meditating,
I am bound to come off badly. It's quite
against my nature to sit still."

WU CHANG-EN

The power of gentleness

In the world there is nothing more submissive and weak than water. Yet for attacking that which is hard and strong nothing can surpass it.

LAO TZU 6TH CENTURY B.C.

Everyone
knows the use
of usefulness;
nobody
understands
the usefulness
of the useless.

CHUANG TZU
369 - 286 B.C.

SUMMER
GRASSES,
ALL THAT
REMAINS
OF SOLDIERS'
DREAMS.

BASHO 1644-1694

WORDS

ARE MERE

BUBBLES OF

WATER,

BUT DEEDS

ARE DROPS

OF GOLD!

AUTHOR UNKNOWN

The one who respects other

I

f you want happiness
for an hour, take a nap.
If you want happiness for a year,
inherit a fortune.
If you want happiness for a lifetime,
help someone.

CHINESE PROVERB

. respected by them.

MENCIUS 372-289 B.C.

The gifts of age

Small understanding doesn't get to where great
understanding gets. Youth doesn't know
what age teaches. How do I know?
The morning mushroom doesn't know
dawn from dusk. The summer cicada knows neither
spring nor autumn. And so it is with youth.

CHUANG TZU 369-286 B.C.

THE ONLY TRUE STRENGTH IS
A STRENGTH THAT PEOPLE DO NOT FEAR.

LAO TZU 6TH CENTURY B.C.

TO KNOW WHAT IS RIGHT
AND NOT DO IT IS THE WORST
COWARDICE.

CONFUCIUS 551-479 B.C.

Even though you have ten thousand fields,
you can only eat one measure of rice a day;
even though your dwelling
contains one thousand rooms, you can only use
eight feet of space at night.

CHINESE WISDOM

The softest things
in the world
overcome the hardest things
in the world.

LAO TZU 6TH CENTURY B.C.

Drinking tea,
eating rice,
I pass my time
as it comes;
Looking down
at the stream,
Looking up
at the mountain,
how serene
and relaxed
I feel indeed!

ZEN POEM

You ask why
I make my home
in the mountain forest,
and I smile,
and am silent,
and even my soul remains quiet:
it lives in the other world
which no one owns.
The peach trees blossom.
The water flows.

LI PO 701-762

The rewards

Under all circumstances,
practise five perfect virtues;
these five things are gravity,
generosity of soul, sincerity,
earnestness and kindness.

CONFUCIUS 551-479 B.C.

of kindness

Kindness in words creates confidence.
Kindness in thinking creates profoundness.
Kindness in giving creates love.

LAO TZU 6TH CENTURY B.C.

Three pillars of wisdom

BRING PEACE TO THE OLD,
HAVE TRUST IN YOUR FRIENDS,
AND CHERISH THE YOUNG.

CONFUCIUS 551-479 B.C.

W hat is well planted cannot be uprooted...
Cultivate virtue in you own person
and it becomes a genuine part of you.
Cultivate it in the family and it will abide.
Cultivate it in the community
and it will live and grow.
Cultivate it in the state and it will
flourish abundantly. Cultivate it in the world
and it will become universal.

LAO TZU 6TH CENTURY B.C.

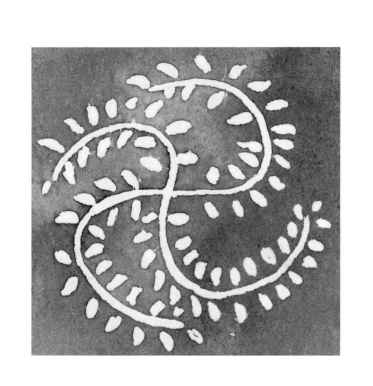

They who know
the truth are not equal
to those who love it,
and they who love it are
not equal to those
who delight in it.

CONFUCIUS 551-479 B.C.

When the sun rises, I go to work.
When the sun goes down,
I take my rest.
I dig the well from which I drink,
I farm the soil which yields my food,
I share creation; kings can do no more.

CHINESE PROVERB

When
I let go
of what
I am,
I become what
I might be.

LAO TZU
6TH CENTURY B.C.